AVADHUT

A Book of Poems

BARKHA

Made with ❤ on the Notion Press Platform

www.notionpress.com

To Maithili, Utkarsh, Ronit, Vishal and Vinay –

May you shine brighter than diamonds.

To Kamla – my grandmother – always stay a child at heart.

To mom and dad –

Explore the world.

and

To my young brothers and sisters around the world who make this world a beautiful place by just being who they are –

Keep learning and growing my friends.

Contents

Foreword

"Growing old is mandatory, but growing up is optional." – Walt Disney

Before you begin this book, I invite you to close your eyes and think of your favourite childhood memory. Picture it vividly—where are you? Who is with you? How do you feel in that moment? Now, ask yourself: what would it take to relive that joy, that innocence, that unfiltered sense of wonder?

I ask this because, as I read Avadhut, a beautiful collection of poems written by my dear friend Barkha, I found myself effortlessly transported back to my own childhood—an era of curiosity, adventure, and boundless imagination.

Although this book is primarily written for children, I truly believe it speaks to readers of all ages:

• To parents, who wish to reconnect with their inner child while creating a warm, nurturing world for their little ones.

• To older siblings, who love, protect, and guide their younger ones through the highs and lows of life.

• To children, whose hearts overflow with wonder, dreams, and endless possibilities.

Each poem in this collection is more than just words on a page; it is an open door to self-reflection, nostalgia, and discovery. Some readers may find a piece of their own childhood in these verses, while others may uncover new perspectives and emotions. The best way to experience this book is to share it —with family, with friends, with anyone who cherishes the magic of childhood.

Barkha and I have been friends since we were an energetic, wide-eyed pair of eight-year-olds. Over the years, I have watched her grow into the kind, compassionate, and remarkable woman she is today. But what I admire most about her is that she never let go of her inner child. She nurtures that part of herself with love, patience, and joy—a quality that shines through in every poem she has written.

Radha Choudhary

Preface

Hello friend! I am Barkha which means rain. You can call me Barkha Didi (Hindi for elder sister). I am the eldest in my home and among all my siblings. I have always tried to be a role model for them and a helping hand just like Pooh was to Winnie, or Patrick was to Spongebob. This year, I realised that not just them, but all my young friends around the world need me. Hence, I wrote my first book ever!

Just like you, I too wanted to be an astronaut when I was an eight-year-old girl when I came to know about Kalpana Chawla – the first woman of Indian origin to be in space. I was highly inspired by her and realized that being a girl means you can do anything, or be anything in the world.

Being the eldest child in the house, I took after my father - to be independent, do things on my own and diligently follow all my pursuits. I believed not asking for help was a sign of bravery and being tough. I observed that my mother worked twice as hard as my father and I learned the virtue of being resilient and managing everything, come what may, from her. But as I grew, I realised we all need help, a friend and sometimes we need to be that person for ourselves and others.

Just like when we throw a stone in still water, it creates waves in concentric circles. Similarly, a little nudge can create a ripple effect for our own personal growth. How would you feel if you had people who tell you don't worry, I would not let you fall? Or someone clapping the loudest for all your achievements and celebrating your uniqueness? Wouldn't we all grow to be more confident and happier?

These poems are written to make all of you feel special. To encourage and motivate you that you are enough, you have all the potential in the world to do what you want and achieve, and to be proud of who you are. The universe is conspiring to give you the best.

I decided to write this book as I realized that being different is okay, that having different interests is fine too. I like swimming, playing volleyball, learning physics, painting, dancing on my favourite songs and yes as a young girl I wanted to be an astronaut. Now, I have an excellent career, I am financially independent and I follow my heart.

The world tried telling me that I have too many interests and I should only follow one, but I realised that I have the capacity to follow each of my hobbies and passions. Let me tell you this, being labelled or confining yourself in a box is fine but if you feel you want to do more in life, learn new art forms, and work on your growth, you are one hundred percent right! You can be anything in this world that you want to be, with determination, diligence and discipline.

Barkha

29.03.2025

Acknowledgments

I would like to thank my guru, Shri Shailendra Sharma, my late mentor Dr. Daisaku Ikeda, my parents, my family and my dear friends, Radha, Vyomi and Shakul for their endless encouragement, enthusiasm and support.

1. The King of Failures

Why does it happen to me?

To God, numerous letters I have mailed.

I start a new journey and evil strikes,

I have lost the count, how many times I have failed.

A fish out of water learns to walk.

I see the opportunity with only a single fin,

Winning is like swimming in stagnant water,

The ocean of failures, makes me win.

2. Sky Is Not the Limit

Dream big! Dream small! Or don't dream at all.

Whose dream to follow, I ponder as I lie on my bed,

Everyone tells me to reach for the skies,

Confused and lost, I sleep with voices in my head.

Grateful to all, but I am unique and me,

I will follow my lead and yours I shall quit.

My ambitions and dreams travel way beyond our galaxies,

The sky is not my limit!

3. I am a Misfit

Listen friends! Listen to me!

I do what my heart orders.

I am a small boat and many storms may come,

I shall sail through to cross all the borders.

Everyone calls me mad,

Small, crooked and not so tall,

But I enter a cave – courageously helping all the big
ships,

A misfit paves the way for all.

4. The Helping Hand

When you expect the least,

The helping hand comes to aid,

The universe comes to help those who help
themselves,

Take a step ahead. Enough said.

The faith is strengthened and you feel a tickle,

The surroundings are same yet you feel new,

Growing like a sprout from a seed,

A mystic bond, those who get you are only a few.

4. My Inner Voice

I see a dream in the mid of the day,

Starkly different from the mundane which makes
me bored.

I am flying in my castle

And I fight a purple dragon with my golden sword.

To be or not to be,

I succumb to the easy decision painstakingly.

One day I shall kill the demon of others will,

For I too want to live deliberately.

CUPCAKE

6. A Good Friend

I am driving with a smile.

Nonstop chatter with my friend on the side.

Even if the car gets punctured,

I am happy to take a stride.

Similar is life with unknown stops

But I have got a listener, a supporter and a guide,

I take great pride to announce that I have

A good friend who makes it a fun ride.

7. A Saviour in Disguise

Walking through the jungle

I forget the way back,

It is getting dark and I see thorny bushes.

Then panic strikes – I wish I had a map.

I see someone walking towards me,

The right way he apprises,

Appearing out of nowhere

God has sent me a saviour in disguise.

8. My Personality is my Strength

The lightning speed of the bolt

Shows the effortless power of electricity.

The water moves through mountains,

Leaving its mark through seasonal cyclicity.

Yes! I am different and unique.

I look at myself in the mirror of full length,

A bouquet of different qualities – I learn.

My personality is my strength.

9. Cosmic Connections

A photograph, a book and a paper.

Reading through the ink – a conversus.

All stardust and maybe more in a different plane,

Yet we are a noscitur a sociis.

There are many like us, yet to arrive at the question,

Is the most difficult part of the equation.

Stop floating and catch a breath,

You already have billions of cosmic connections.

10. My Mission in Life

When you find me shivering in the rain,

And perspirating red sweat in the scorching sun,

Do not underestimate me,

Even without my shoes, miles I run.

I make my own path with the sword of my
discipline,

Yet anyone can disarm me and create strife

But I promise that I will stay true

To my mission in life.

I am a winner!

11. Celebrate Yourself

Like the rainbow shines after rain,

Clap for yourself and dance.

Sing and create symphonies,

This is your chance.

Learn to pat your own back,

You are a queen, a hero, a saviour.

Only you know what it takes to be you,

Celebrating yourself is the ultimate best human
behaviour.